Ofelia Castañeda López
Johnny Leobardo González Pérez

A WEB site for Mexican coastal lagoons.

Ofelia Castañeda López
Johnny Leobardo González Pérez

A WEB site for Mexican coastal lagoons.

Design, construction and structure for the transmission of diagnostic information and scientific studies.

ScienciaScripts

Imprint

Any brand names and product names mentioned in this book are subject to trademark, brand or patent protection and are trademarks or registered trademarks of their respective holders. The use of brand names, product names, common names, trade names, product descriptions etc. even without a particular marking in this work is in no way to be construed to mean that such names may be regarded as unrestricted in respect of trademark and brand protection legislation and could thus be used by anyone.

Cover image: www.ingimage.com

This book is a translation from the original published under ISBN 978-620-2-13099-8.

Publisher:
Sciencia Scripts
is a trademark of
Dodo Books Indian Ocean Ltd. and OmniScriptum S.R.L publishing group

120 High Road, East Finchley, London, N2 9ED, United Kingdom
Str. Armeneasca 28/1, office 1, Chisinau MD-2012, Republic of Moldova, Europe
Printed at: see last page
ISBN: 978-620-3-59400-3

CONTENT

DEDICATION

To my son Daniel, who has been my inspiration to complete this work and to be an example for him to follow.

To my partner Sandra Nayeli who, together with my son Daniel, has supported me, and with many sacrifices and patiently waited for me.

To my parents, Leobardo González Cantero and Belem Pérez Salcedo, who have always supported me unconditionally, who sacrificed themselves to give me an education and who, with determination and tenacity, never took their finger off the scale so that I could complete a professional career.

To my sisters Belem and Jenny González Pérez, who have always been willing and never hesitated to offer me their unconditional support.

To my teachers, who worked hard to make their teachings bear fruit and succeed.

To my friends, who always encouraged me.

ACKNOWLEDGEMENTS

I would like to thank my teachers at the Instituto Tecnológico de Iztapalapa and, in particular, I would like to thank Lic. Orquídea Acevedo Calderón for her advice in the preparation of this work.

I would like to thank Ofelia Castañeda López, head of the CDELM, Department of Hydrobiology at the UAM Iztapalapa, for the facilities she provided me with and her support in order to carry out my Professional Residency in her area with the development of the website design.

I would also like to thank the Universidad Autónoma Metropolitana, Unidad Iztapalapa, for opening its doors to me and providing me with the space to do my Professional Residency at this Institution through the offices of Social Service and Professional Internships in order to create the link and open the agreement with the Instituto Tecnológico de Iztapalapa.

To my parents Belem and Leobardo, my recognition and gratitude always, for guiding me on the right path, for instilling values in me, for their love, patience and understanding.

I would also like to thank those who helped me to obtain materials and bibliographies.

My thanks to all those who, in one way or another, have supported me over the years so that I was able to realise my professional career with this work. There are not enough words to express my gratitude, appreciation and affection.

SUMMARY

The coastal zone, from the perspective of its ecological study, represents a challenge, since a mosaic of habitats, ecosystems, biotopes and ecotones are located in this wide strip of land. The interaction of the sea with the wetlands and the characteristics of the latter form a complex object of study, where the analysis of each of its components and an integral vision of the ecosystem are essential elements for the understanding and interpretation of the diverse phenomena that occur there.Coastal plains are the result of numerous factors ranging from local climatology and its water cycle, to complex biological and adaptive mechanisms of aquatic organisms, to complicated processes for the reuse of biogenic materials. Thus, it is of little benefit to propose programmes and eventual solutions aimed exclusively at the coastline without understanding and comprehending the phenomena that occur in the uplands, when it is precisely their runoff that is one of the causes of the origin of these plains. In Mexico, these interactions, together with its geographical position, have resulted in the creation of ecosystems of high ecological and productive value, including floodplains, marshes and coastal lagoons.However, there is no adequate planning or policy specifically aimed at the conservation and/or exploitation of these resources. This is the result of the fact that, on the one hand, knowledge about this problem has been limited to scientific research, mainly led by higher education institutions or research centres, and secondly, that projects and programmes initiated by the government sector have underestimated the interaction with the scientific community.With this in mind, the present project consists of the development of a web-based digital consultation system that uses new technologies to improve the consultation process at the Universidad Autónoma Metropolitana. The objective of this is to provide complete and updated information on coastal ecosystems through the Mexican Coastal Ecosystems Documentation Centre (CDELM), as well as to provide a series of functionalities to teachers and students who consult the site. Nowadays, websites are of vital importance and indispensable for accessing specialised information, as they make it possible to disseminate it more widely. This project was developed using html5, css, javascript, and php technologies, which effectively served to compile all the CDELM information with its respective guidelines.

INTRODUCTION

The study of coastal ecosystems is complex, as they are the result of the interaction of multiple natural factors: the input of freshwater from upland rivers, the input of seawater due to tides and the opening of inlets or mouths in water bodies, regional climatic variations, biological particularities such as halophytic vegetation, variable sedimentation rates dependent on coastal dynamics, and recently, the effect of anthropogenic modifications and activities.Despite the budgetary limitations that have occurred in the scientific research sector, there is a continuation and generation of projects to learn about the natural resources existing in coastal ecosystems and to implement new measures for their use and management, for which different instances in some coastal regions of Mexico have contributed with important advances in the knowledge of these ecosystems, mainly those with high economic and ecological potential.

Based on the importance of coastal ecosystems in Mexico, this thesis presents a partial analysis of the availability of information on the state of knowledge of coastal water bodies on both coasts, through the collection of specialised literature for the construction and improvement of an updated website for consultation of reference sources, characteristics and description of the coastal ecosystems existing in Mexico.

From a Web client, all usable information is seen as a "flat universe" in which most of the data is accessible in a few clicks, hiding a web of details needed to access the data. However, there is a structure of configured computers running applications that store and exchange information. In this respect, a clear distinction should be made between the Internet and the World Wide Web (WWW); the latter is just one of the information services found on the Internet, whose network of computers communicate via the TCP/IP protocol. The evolution of the use of web browsers as an interface facilitates access to many Internet services.

The Web project has based its success on a very appropriate design of its elements, making it suitable for the construction of complex information systems due to its relative simplicity, since it is based on a client-server model in which information exchanges between servers and clients are carried out through simple requests.

HTTP servers are the centre of the information distribution system. On them, clients enter URLs (Universal Resource Locator), which are very similar to the paths to a document in the directory structure of a computer and which also contain the Internet address of the computer providing the document. This process locates the original copy of the documents to be distributed so that clients have the facility to collect them.

Web clients are responsible for collecting information from servers and displaying it in the most convenient way, therefore, a terminal or device is required for each working environment. However, as discussed below, the capabilities of Web clients can be more extensive.

JUSTIFICATION

Mexico has 1,567,000 ha of estuarine surfaces. The Pacific has an average of 892,800 ha and the Gulf of Mexico no less than 674,500 ha. Estuarine waters can be defined as those aquatic surfaces where there is a mixture of water coming from continental runoff and oceanic water through the tidal phenomenon. The term estuary comes from the word aeustus meaning tidal. Coastal estuarine ecosystems stand out for their intrinsic importance for the numerous species that inhabit them, either temporarily or permanently (Contreras and Castañeda, 2004).

The WWW brings together several aspects that make it an attractive and promising technology, because it is a hypertext system that makes it possible to jump from one page to another very easily through links. It can also be considered a multimedia system, as it mixes text with graphics and objects in other formats (essentially images, sounds and videos), as well as being able to run applications. In the past, it was a system that made it possible to surf the net and get the best out of the various Internet services, as well as making documentation available on a private network in an inexpensive and attractive way. Nowadays it is a medium that allows the execution of multiple applications, however, it maintains its functionality and the characteristics of universality and free of charge. The Internet is universal because WWW pages are available to any type of connected device and user. As part of this universality one could include the equality of the network that gives the same status of a private server to the server of a large company with several pages and a huge development team. Another important element is simplicity, so it is aimed at any type of user, whether computer literate or not, so it is relatively easy to use. To achieve this element, the WWW uses hypermedia techniques which allow text, images, animations, sounds and videos to be included from within a document. In such a way, documents can be easily linked to each other regardless of their location.

Based on the information analysed and summarised about Mexico's coastal resources, which will be contained on the CDELM website, the authors consider that progress in the knowledge of these ecosystems has prospered significantly in the last thirty years and that the quantity and quality of research and information is excellent, in general terms, so that new computer and storage technologies can be used to contribute to decision-making aimed at the conservation, regeneration, use or management of these resources, so that the information is available to any user.This project arises from the need to create a website that functions as a database and links the sectors interested in basic information on coastal ecosystems in Mexico. It is intended that the website will serve as a support for scientific research, as well as for decision-makers in the governmental sector and bodies dedicated to the management of coastal ecosystems. It is intended that the CDELM website of the UAMI concentrates as much information as possible on the knowledge and current affairs of coastal ecosystems, so that, by having a large capacity for viewing files, a website represents a strength to face international competition in specific areas that require great technological breadth.

OBJECTIVES

General

•Design, build and develop a website for the CDELM that allows free access to general and specialised information on estuarine coastal ecosystems.

Specific

•Design and structure a database with diagnostic information and scientific studies based on a web search glossary that directs the user to the documentary collection on the management of Mexico's coastal ecosystems.

•To build a website whose structure provides specialised and scientific information that is easy to access, based on the visualisation and conceptualisation of the problems and alternatives for the use and management of the coastal zone and its ecosystems.

•Convey the functionality of the website to users so that they can recognise the coastal zone and its ecosystems as a natural, ecologically and economically manageable entity.

CHAPTER 1

GENERAL

1.1 What is CDELM?

Given the need to contribute to the ecological planning and management of the Mexican coasts, collaboration with different academic institutions to share the information generated by scientific research groups specialised in ecology, biology, conservation and management of coastal ecosystems and their hydrobiological resources has been essential, which led to the founding of the Documentation Centre of Mexican Coastal Ecosystems (CDELM) in 1989, which belongs to the Department of Hydrobiology of the Autonomous Metropolitan University-Universidad Iztapalapa. This is an academic project founded in 1989 by the members of the Laboratory of Coastal Ecosystems (formerly Oceanography), which aims to gather all existing information on Mexican coastal resources.

Much of the objective information is dispersed or inaccessible, in particular, marine and/or coastal sciences in Mexico have a relatively low number of publications available on the different characteristics of coastal ecosystems, because it was not until the 1960s that the specialised study of coastal and estuarine ecosystems became more relevant to the scientific community.

The CDELM has been dedicated to gathering, cataloguing and capturing dispersed information, taking into account rigorous criteria for the review and selection of information, so that most, or all, of the information available in its database comes from scientific articles, both national and international, theses of different academic degrees and reports of participations in events. specialised. The CDELM is made up of an information collection of approximately 5400 bibliographic references (including abstracts) on all the scientific topics published on Mexican coastal ecosystems.

The following is a general description of the CDELM:
•Name of the institution:
Documentation Centre for Mexican Coastal Ecosystems (CDELM).
Department of Hydrobiology, Area of Coastal Ecosystems, Division of
Biological and Health Sciences. Autonomous Metropolitan University,
Iztapalapa Unit. RFC of the company: UAM-740101AR1

•Mission:
To promote and strengthen activities that bring the results of research at
UAM Iztapalapa closer to the public and private productive sectors in
order to contribute to the well-being of society and the country's
competitiveness.

•Vision:
Normalise, standardise, regulate and promote the transfer processes of
innovative knowledge generated at UAM Iztapalapa, through a single
office that serves researchers and the public and private sectors
interested in specialised information, protecting, in the first instance, the
knowledge to be commercialised.

The UAM Iztapalapa has consolidated itself as the promoter of the
capacities of this academic unit, establishing a reliable relationship
between the productive sectors and the University. The CDELM is an
office that acts with transparency and vision, contributing to the social
commitment of UAM Iztapalapa.

•Location and contact details:
San Rafael Atlixco 186, Vicentina, Iztapalapa C.P. 09340 Mexico City.
Telephone: 5804-4745 y 46. Responsible: Mtra. en Educación Ambiental
Ofelia Castañeda López, email: clo@xanum.uam.mx

•Turn:
The task of the Department of Hydrobiology lies in articulating the links in
a chain that goes from description to the generation of information and
technology aimed at its object of study, which includes the
hydrobiological resources of aquatic ecosystems (UAM, 2014).

Figure 1. Location of the CDELM, Dept. of Hydrobiology, UAM Iztapalapa.

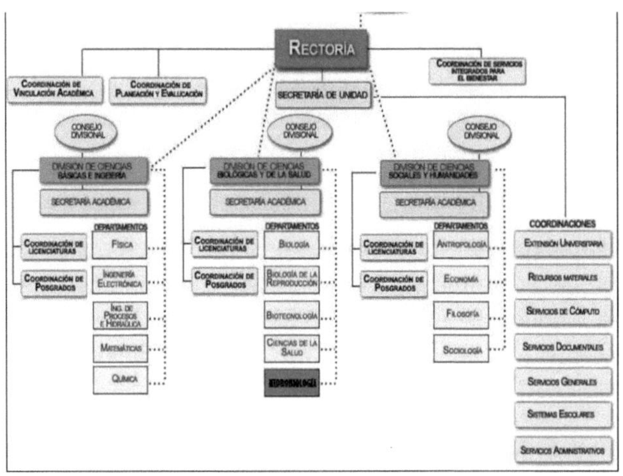

Figure 2. Organisational chart of the Institution and CDELM step.

1.2 Reference framework of project

1.2.1 Approach of the problem

Thanks to the study and field monitoring of Mexican coastal ecosystems, it has been possible to identify the need for a virtual medium to facilitate access to the information generated on these ecosystems and to share the progress of the scientific community in order to promote academic training with greater scope and competitiveness in the areas covered by the Department of Hydrobiology.

Although the Autonomous Metropolitan University is known for the technological tools at its disposal, it lacks a technological means that would promote its progress and innovations in the Documentation Centre for Mexican Coastal Ecosystems (CDELM). For the CDELM it is relevant to solve the information problem in the area and considers the following actions to be necessary:

• Implement and/or enable an internet site so that users can locate the required information on the current state of coastal ecosystems, in this way UAM will be a leading institution in specialised research on coastal and hydrobiological resources.

• Opt for dissemination programmes on the use of information technologies for knowledge and research in the area of coastal ecosystems aimed at the university community and the general public to facilitate access to information more easily.

1.2.2 Scope of the project

This project will enable the university community and the general public, mainly the education sector, to do the following:

• Know and understand the advances of new information technologies and their impact on research on Mexican coastal ecosystems.

• Use technological tools to have quick and up-to-date access to data and information contained in the CDELM databases.

• Provide CDELM with search preference data to improve the structure of the website and offer a better experience in the consultation of information through the use of virtual tools.

• Use the information contained in the CDELM and apply the knowledge acquired in specialised work and scientific dissemination and popularisation.

• Update previous knowledge of coastal ecosystems and consult their current status based on the collection of current information contained in the CDELM.

• To enable students, teachers and researchers to gain a better understanding of the processes, projects and events occurring in coastal ecosystems.

The purpose of this project is to provide the CDELM with a virtual tool that will enable it to improve communication between the academic community and promote it nationally and internationally, making appropriate use of existing technological communication resources. As well as streamlining pedagogical processes and strengthening teaching skills and abilities by using virtual media to enhance their performance and improve teaching activities. With the implementation of this project, the aim is to directly benefit the university community of UAM Iztapalapa in order to promote communication between the groups that comprise it and other higher education and research institutions.

1.2.3 Limitations

Due to the objectives of this project, the time frame for the construction of the website, which will be a maximum of 6 months, and the amount of resources available in the Coastal Ecosystems Area are considered as limitations. In addition, the maintenance of the website was not contemplated, other than its design, construction and initial operation, which will affect the operation of the site in the future, since only the development of the interface is foreseen without considering the catalogue of images, the validation of social network accounts and micro blogs, in general. Another important limitation is the lack of staff dedicated to the development of this project, which results in fewer processes being carried out.

CHAPTER 2

THEORETICAL FRAMEWORK

2.1 General overview of coastal ecosystems

A coastal ecosystem is a set of natural factors (system) in which physico-chemical variables interact, such as oxygen, temperature, nutrients, salinity, among others, and biological factors, such as populations and communities of different types of organisms and their biological processes. Each of the individuals belonging to the ecosystem fulfils a function necessary for the ecosystem to maintain its conditions and the particularities of the ecological niche.

Coastal ecosystems are highly productive and have been extensively studied by the scientific community. The primary productivity of coastal ecosystems forms the basis of the food chain. In addition, coastal plains are the result of numerous factors where they are involved from the local climatology and its water cycle, to complex biological and adaptive mechanisms of aquatic organisms, to complicated processes for the reuse of biogenic materials.It is of little benefit to propose programmes and eventual solutions aimed exclusively at the coastline without understanding and comprehending the phenomena that occur in the highlands, when it is precisely their runoff that is one of the causes of the origin of these plains. In Mexico, these interactions, together with its geographical position, have resulted in the creation of ecosystems of high ecological and productive value, including floodplains, marshes and coastal lagoons.The coastal zone, from the perspective of its ecological study, represents a challenge, since a mosaic of habitats, ecosystems, biotopes and ecotones are located in this wide strip of land. The interaction of the sea with the wetlands and the characteristics of the latter form a complex object of study, where the analysis of each of its components and an integral vision of the ecosystem are essential elements for the understanding and interpretation of the diverse phenomena that occur there. Nowadays, in order to be at the forefront, it is important to take into account the importance and boom of websites to disseminate and publicise the pedagogical processes that are carried out in educational institutions and to exchange new advances in research, among other things (Contreras-Espinosa, 2010).

2.2 What is the World Wide Web?

The World Wide Web, or WWW, is "the web that covers the world", the aggregation of all information available on the Internet that can be accessed through a web browser. For this purpose, it is common to use the terms Web, WWW or World Wide Web.

For Internet pages there are writing systems called "mark-up language". HTML (Hypertext Markup Language) is the most widely used; with this language, commands are sent so that information is presented in browsers to display web pages. The well-known tags make it possible to format the document and combine it with other multimedia elements.

Table 1. Definitions of the elements of the WWW (World Wide Web)

HTTP protocol	It was created to enable hypertext, hyperlinks and hypermedia to do their job. The acronym stands for Hypertext Transfer Protocol.It works in four basic steps: connection, request, response and disconnection.Considered a stateless protocol, because it does not store information about the transactions it makes.
Browsers	To surf the internet you need a programme that can access the web pages, these are Programmes can be found at called browsers; the more
	are Internet Explorer, Mozilla Firefox and Google Chrome.
URL addressing	It is used to name the location of the information to be accessed on the Internet through a standard character system. Every information resource on the web has a unique URL. With this address, the browser accesses the page and displays it on the screen.
Search engines	To find the desired data if the URL is not known, search servers or search engines are used. The most popular search engines are Google and Yahoo.

Each object that is embedded in a web page is a separate file from the page itself, i.e. only files are linked. A link is said to be broken when a web page cannot retrieve some of the objects it had embedded, or when a hyperlink is not properly configured. Typical elements presented on a website are text, graphics, photographs, animations, video and audio.

2.3   HyperText Markup Language 5 System (HTML5)

Nowadays it is essential to recognise the importance of websites to disseminate updated information and to know the advances applied and/or used in the educational area and in research on Mexican coastal ecosystems. Regarding the use of technologies, html5 is not so different from what is already known.as HyperText Markup Language or HyperText Markup Language, the difference is that html5 is defined as a group of technologies that work together to solve a given purpose. The three technologies used under this name are html5, css3, and JavaScript; most of these technologies are considered Font-end as they are used for programming directly with the user or client.

Using html5 it is possible to create sites without programming knowledge, since it is possible to use content management systems (CMS). However, in the particular case of this project for the use of UAM Iztapalapa, it is considered that the use of this technology is not viable due to the limitations it implies. Therefore, it is intended to use html5 technology to develop the main structure of the website using tags for text and images as headers and other elements. In addition, text editors, such as notepad++ or Sublime Text, can be used to directly manipulate the HTML5 code.

- Basic example of html5 tag work (Taken from w3schools, 2016).

```
<HTML>
    <HEAD>
        <TITLE>P&aacute;gina de ejemplo</TITLE>
    </HEAD>
    <BODY>
        <H2> Encabezado </H2>
        <P>Primer p&aacute;rrafo debajo del encabezado.</P>
        <H3> Un encabezado <BR> en dos renglones </H3>
        <P>P&aacute;rrafo con partes <B>en negrita</B> </P>
    </BODY> </HTML>
```

On the other hand, CSS or cascading style sheets is a language for creating presentations of a document previously structured with HTML.

Table 2. CSS (cascading style sheets) versions and their specifications.

Version	Specifications
CSS 1	Font properties: type, size and emphasis Colour of text, backgrounds, borders or other elements Text attributes such as word spacing, letter spacing, line spacing, etc. Alignment of texts, images, tables or others Box properties such as margin, border, padding or spacing List identification and presentation properties
CSS 2	Functionalities own of the layers (<div>) such as relative/absolute/fixed positioning, levels (z-index), etc. Concept of "media types Support for auditory style sheets Two-way text, shadows, etc.
CSS 2.1	Fixes some bugs found in CSS2 Removes poorly supported or inoperable features in browsers
CSS 3	Divided into separate documents called "modules Preserves CSS2 features to maintain compatibility, but adds new features per module.

As with all websites created for any type of business or institution, i.e. those in which digital images and text sections are created or manipulated, depending on the nature of the medium, an intuitive user interface is created, keeping users engaged with the site.

- Example from use basic of CSS (w3schools, 2016).

```css
Body {
    Background-color: #180A0A;
}

h1 {
    text-shadow: 0 5px 3px #CCC;
    color: #000;
    font-size: 40px;
}

h2 {
    text-shadow: 0 5px 3px #CCC;
    color: #000;
    font-size: 40px;
}

p {
    font-family:"Times New Roman"
    font-size: 40px;
}
```

2.4 Responsive design

New technological advances can be seen in ICTs, since it is possible to view any web content on any type of device, from desktop computers, tablets and mobiles. It is considered that the use of information technologies (ICTs) should be fundamental for education, because the consultation of information in digital media is becoming more relevant every day and increases the competitiveness and labour or educational productivity of users who use them. Responsive design is a technique that helps to maintain the correct visualisation of the same page, responding to the need for a given website to adapt to current devices.

This technique is characterised because the layouts (contents) and images are fluid and because it uses the CSS3 media-queries code. It also allows resizing and positioning the elements of the web in such a way that they adapt to the width of each device, which allows the user to access a better user experience; as well as reducing development time and avoiding duplicate content, because the files can be shared more quickly and easily. In this way, it is possible to provide the same website content to all users and offer a better consultation and/or development experience, compared to other approaches to web development, in the creation of mobile apps, domain variation or dynamic websites depending on the terminal.

Figure 3. Key features of Responsive Design.

Figure 4. Presentation of Responsive Design on a website.

2.5 Interactions with JavaScript and jQuery

The system or website needs to interact with HTML documents, handle animations, schedule events and manipulate the DOM (Document Object Modeling), for this purpose, JavaScript or jQuery is formed, which allow improvements in the user interface and get a better dynamic web page. In this regard, JavaScript is an interpreted language that was developed for use in web browsers. JQuery is a developed and specific library of JavaScript code that is used to simplify some processes such as menu correction, image docking, document scrolling and event manipulation (JavaScript, 2016).

2.6 Hypertext PreProcessor (PHP)

The Hypertext PreProcessor or PHP is a general purpose programming language suitable for website development. If a server-side programming language is used as the back-end programming, it allows to have control over the more dynamic content of the website such as sending emails, visitor control, or data manipulation (PHP, 2016). Communication on a website takes place in a key dimension, i.e. directly, so the creation of interactive media using this technology would allow an educational institution to have one-way knowledge-oriented tools that facilitate the training of students in a dynamic way.

2.7   WAMP Server

Wamp Server is a free tool for Windows, a must-have for every website developer. It provides support for frontend or backend developers, allowing them to create applications with Apache, PHP and Base with MySQL. At the same time, it allows uploading HTML pages with CSS and JavaScript, making possible a development environment necessary to manage the local server configuration, as well as debugging tests of code written to improve handling, so that the browser can interpret it. In addition, it contains a PHP MyAdmin database manager that can be used to create new databases, query them, generate SQL scripts, and export or import databases or tables. The use of this technology in this project will consist in the evaluation of the evolution and continuity of the site, which will allow it to be executed locally before uploading it to a hosting.

Figure 6. Wamp Server Services logos.

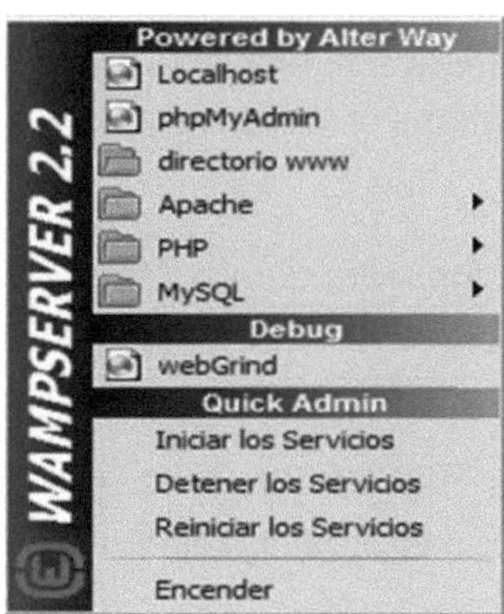

Figure 7. Installation of the Wamp Server.

CHAPTER 3

METHODOLOGY

3.1 Website design

Web pages are designed to contain all kinds of information, so that elegant multimedia presentations of all possible contents can be constructed. The work programme of this project, as mentioned above, contemplates the creation of a website with sufficient capacity to display basic data or characteristic information concerning the coastal ecosystems of Mexico, which will belong to the Department of Hydrobiology of the UAM Iztapalapa.

In the following, in simplified form, the steps to follow for the creation, operation and demonstration of a web page written with HTML are listed (WAMP, 2016):

•They offer the user the possibility to trigger a URL, either by selecting a link from a document or by entering it directly into the browser.

•They decode the fields of a URL.
•They connect to the corresponding server, to collect the content of the URL.

•They interpret the hypertext and display it, according to the characteristics and limitations of the environment in which the device is running.

•They collect the rest of the components of a web page, such as: images, sounds, Java applications, flash animations, embedded objects, etc.

•After activation of a link, they identify the status of the required information, and the above process is repeated.

•They often have utilities, which reduce many operations such as: temporary copies of recently visited pages, URL schedules, e-mail clients, etc.

In addition, the use of Information Architecture (IA) is also proposed to improve the consultation and design processes of the application. Below is a description of the methodology that defines four essential phases in the development of a website:

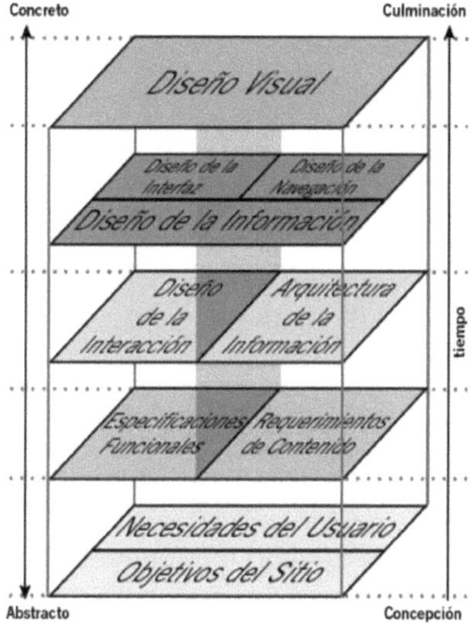

Figure 8. Overall scheme of the Information Architecture (Garret, 2011).

3.2 Website needs and requirements

Due to the type of website being planned, functionalities will be developed that describe in detail the different contents to be included in the reference library. Therefore, the site will be structured with the following buttons or sections to improve interaction with the user: Home Page, CDELM Objectives, Publications, Collaborations, Services, Who we are and Contact. In the services section, there will be six subcategories: Gallery, Database, Direct Contact, Site Map, Projects and Web Administration.

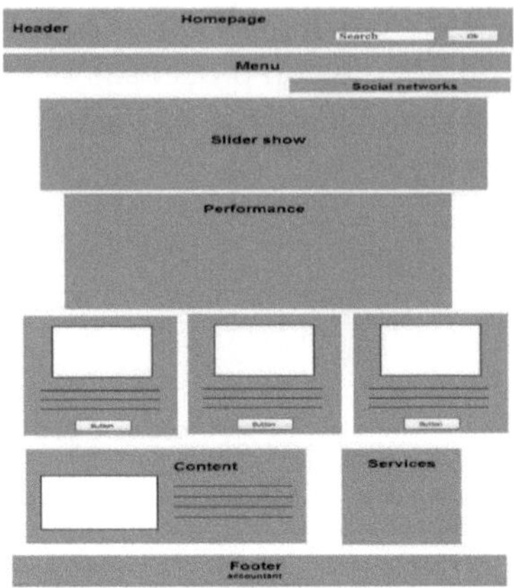

Figure 9. Sketch of the homepage of the CDELM website, UAM Iztapalapa.

The design of the main page of the website shall be displayed in such a way that the system is easily understandable to the user with the intention that during its construction it is understood by the developer in order to avoid errors. In addition, the main interface shall be designed to facilitate future corrections to the website, or the creation of new content or new pages containing the same type of information. The services shall be accounted for in order to maintain the orderliness of the information during navigation on the web consultation site.

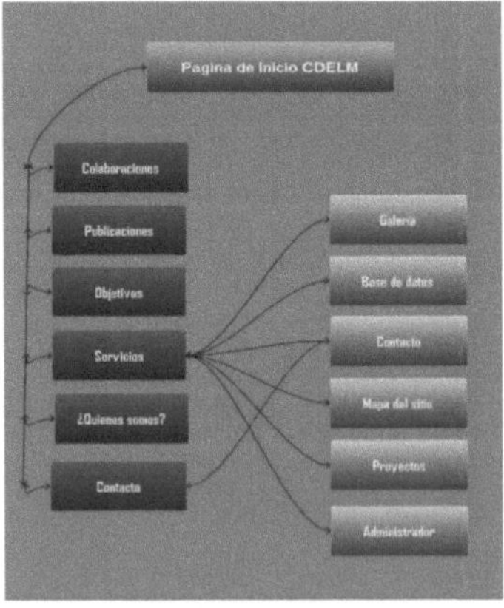

Figure 10. Navigation Map according to the website design envisaged for this project.

The graphic or visual design of a website should reinforce the decisions made by the IA (Information Architecture) and clarify the structure, navigation and consultation of the content. The visual aspects of a website should not only be decorative, but should pursue an objective such as offering an intuitive environment that conveys quality, trust and truthfulness, as well as being a space in which the user feels comfortable. Graphic design, as an emotional symptom, has a very important role to play with the user. This methodology is based on that developed by Garret (2011), in which IA is based on a visual language for descriptive architecture diagrams and navigation flows, which are a standard for prototyping tasks. In order to find out which sectors would use the CDELM website based on different research or knowledge generation interests, a series of surveys were carried out on technology applied to educational resources as a generator of knowledge, to identify the needs of the website that will contain information on Mexican coastal ecosystems and the needs of users when using it. The field research was carried out at UAM Iztapalapa with a sample of 50 people who were asked the following questions (Table 3):

Table 3. Questions from the surveys applied at UAM Iztapalapa.
COMPOSITION OF THE SURVEYS
1. *Do you own a computer or mobile device with internet?*

2. *Do you use the internet frequently?*

3. *Do you think there is a difference between a computer website and a mobile website?*
4. *Do you consider it necessary to implement a website with information on Mexican Coastal Ecosystems?*
5. *Would you like to access the Mexican Coastal Ecosystems Documentation Centre (CDELM) online?*
6. *Through the implementation of the site, do you think that students and teachers would improve communication with CDELM or Mexican Coastal Ecosystems specialists at UAM Iztapalapa?*
7. *Would you like to download or view online the documents concerning Mexican Coastal Ecosystems?*
8. *What do you think a consultation website should look like?*

9. *What features of a website most appeal to you?*

4.1 Survey registration

Based on the answers obtained during the application of the surveys, the following records were obtained with which it was possible to identify some particular needs or characteristics to improve the browsing experience on the CDELM website:

1. Do you own a computer or mobile device with internet?

Variable	Sample	Frequency	Percentage
Yes	50	45	90%
No	50	5	10%

2. Do you use the internet frequently?

Variable	Sample	Frequency	Percentage
Yes	50	46	92%
No	50	4	8%

3. Do you think there is a difference between a computer website and a mobile website?

Variable	Sample	Frequency	Percentage
Yes	50	30	60%
No	50	20	40%

4. Do you consider it necessary to implement a website with information on Mexican Coastal Ecosystems?

Variable	Sample	Frequency	Percentage
Yes	50	49	98%
No	50	1	2%

5. Would you like to access the Mexican Coastal Ecosystems Documentation Centre (CDELM) online?

Variable	Sample	Frequency	Percentage
Yes	50	49	98%
No	50	1	2%

6. Through the implementation of the site, do you think that students and teachers would improve communication with CDELM or Mexican Coastal Ecosystems specialists at UAM Iztapalapa?

Variable	Sample	Frequency	Percentage
Yes	50	49	98%
No	50	2	2%

7. Would you like to download or view online the documents concerning Mexican Coastal Ecosystems?

Variable	Sample	Frequency	Percentage
Yes	50	50	100%
No	50	0	0%

8. What do you think a consultation website should look like?

Variable	Sample	Frequency	Percentage
Image gallery	50	18	36%

9. What features of a website most appeal to you?

Variable	Sample	Frequency	Percentage
Specialised search engine	50	18	36%
Intuitive navigation	50	4	8%
No advertising	50	2	4%
Microblogging or social networking	50	8	16%

4.2 Reference library archives

Based on the collection of information, which will be contained in the website to be developed, the following content was registered for inclusion:Of the 5203 bibliographic references that have been located to date, 2315 correspond to the Gulf of Mexico (44.7%) and 2888 to the Pacific (55.3%). The distribution of the information found for the 17 coastal states, as well as the percentage that each entity represents at the national level, can be reviewed in table 4.

Table 4. Scientific references that address some aspect of the Coastal Ecosystems of the Mexican Republic.

State		# of references	%
1	Veracruz	1197	23.01
2	Baja California Sur	821	15.78
3	Baja California	711	13.67
4	Campeche	518	9.96
5	Sinaloa	439	8.44
6	Sonora	291	5.59
7	Tabasco	178	3.42
8	Guerrero	155	2.98
9	Quintana Roo	149	2.86
10	Yucatan	148	2.84
11	Oaxaca	136	2.61
12	Tamaulipas	125	2.40
13	Jalisco	122	2.34
14	Nayarit	96	1.85
15	Chiapas	66	1.27
16	Colima	44	0.85
17	Michoacán	7	0.13
TOTAL		5203	100

Table 5. Image files counted by section included in the CDELM website.

Image files	
Section	Quantity
Birds	223
Bentos	446
Ecosystems	96
Phytoplankton	101
Fish	413
Vegetation	160
Zooplankton	122
Total	1561

4.3 Website development

As a result of the design, structuring and construction of the CDELM website, it was finalised considering the design and architecture needs. It is considered that the website launched has mainly benefited the teaching and student community, especially those belonging to the Department of Hydrobiology, as it has recently functioned as a didactic and support tool for students, as well as representing a technological space for research activities in Mexican Coastal Ecosystems. Also, it was possible to recognise that there will be greater dissemination of the CDELM and its activities and contents, through a pilot test carried out by the developer, due to the contents of the website and its design. The sections proposed above were created and these improved the distribution of information and facilitated access to the archives of the reference library. Below are some of the most important aspects that resulted from the development of the CDELM website: In addition, the importance of this site lies primarily in the dissemination of the information available on Mexican Coastal Ecosystems, which is why it includes a distribution map of the ecosystems that are studied in Mexico and for which there are scientific references included on the CDELM website. This section can be used in conjunction with the site's search system to find information on a specific topic.

According to the analysis carried out, the need for the area of the Documentation Centre for Mexican Coastal Littoral Ecosystems (or CDELM) is to implement a website that contributes to strengthening communication and learning in the educational community, as well as meeting the demands of the current era in terms of the incorporation of new technologies and dynamics in this area of research. Thus, with the development of the website, it was possible to develop the competences of the Coastal Ecosystems Area to communicate current and specialised information to the student community of UAM Iztapalapa and other institutions. The technologies used for the development of this project were implemented manually, leaving aside the CMS (Web Content Management System) in order to optimise and improve efficiency and reduce response times, debugging the code to obtain a quick response.

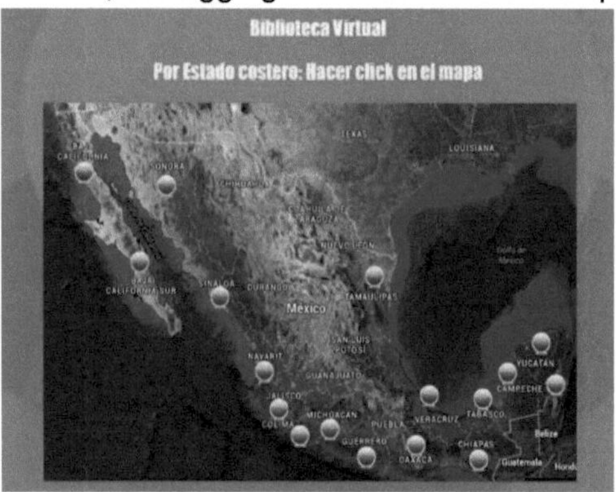

Figure 20. Map of the database for available information on coastal ecosystems organised by state.

Figure 21. Gallery of images in which information can be found on the species that inhabit coastal ecosystems.

CHAPTER 5
CONCLUSIONS

5.1 Conclusions and recommendations

The Centro de Documentación de Ecosistemas Litorales Mexicanos (CDELM) of the Universidad Autónoma Metropolitana de Iztapalapa (UAMI) now has a virtual technological tool that will allow the application of new teaching-learning methodologies, so that teachers and students can access information easily and quickly from any device. Likewise, it is of vital importance that the website is periodically analysed and updated to maintain its users, improve access to information and increase the opportunities for dissemination of specific knowledge on Mexican Littoral Ecosystems. Therefore, it is also recommended to train the staff that manages the website in order to favour the updating processes and maintain good performance and functioning, as well as to train teachers on the functioning of the website and its advantages.

5.2 Competences developed and/or applied

Following an engineering approach, a website was developed with high standards of quality and control with efficient techniques that provides the expected results, using cutting-edge technology that is useful for solving problems in science and education. The skills to analyse, use, design and implement Information Technologies were developed, understanding and solving in an innovative, dynamic and creative way problems of the institution, in this case, UAM Iztapalapa. Although web-focused graphic design is a challenge, it was possible to develop the website without major difficulties. Key actions for website design and development were also identified, such as understanding the client's needs, determining the target audience and establishing effective communication all the way through to pilot testing and delivery of the new site.

SOURCES AND REFERENCES

Cabello-Orós, J. C. (2011). Web design with XHTML, JavaScript and CSS (3rd ed.). Alfaomega, Ra-Ma.

Contreras-Espinosa,F.(2010). Ecosystems Coastal Ecosistemas Costeros Mexicanos: An update. UAM-Iztapalapa.

Díaz, P., Montero-Moreno, S., & Aedo, I. (2005). Web engineering and design patterns. Pearson Prentice Hall.

Garret, J. J. (2011). The elements of the user experience: user-centered design for the web and beyond (2nd ed.). New Riders Publishing.

IBM (2015). IBM SPSS software. https://www.ibm.com/mx-es/spss JavaScript. (2016). Interactions with JavaScript y jQuery. https://www.javascript.com/resources

Krick, E. V. (1972). Introduction to Engineering and Project Engineering (1st ed.). LIMUSA-WILEY S.A.

Pavón, J. (2011). Creating a portal with PHP and MySQL (4th ed.). Alfaomega.
Pérez-López, C. (2003). Administración de sitios y Páginas Web con Macromedia Dreamweaver MX (1st ed.). Alfaomega.

PHP.(2016). Hypertext Preprocessor (PHP).http://php.net/manual/es/intro- whatis.php

Roldán-Martínez, D., Valderas-Aranda, P. J., & Pastor-López, O. (2010). Web applications: A practical approach (1st. ed.). RA-MA S.A. Editorial y Publicaciones.

Shulz, R. G. (2009). Web Design with CSS (1st ed.). Alfaomega.
Soria, R. (1998). Navegar en internet HTML 4: Diseño y creación de páginas web (1st ed.). RA-MA S.A. Editorial y Publicaciones.

Universidad Autónoma Metropolitana (UAM Iztapalapa). (2014). http://www.izt.uam.mx/

Villeta-Molineaux, J. (2000). Design of engineering projects (1st ed.). Instituto Tecnológico de Santo Domingo.

w3schools.(2016). Decoration with leaves from style sheets CSS3.
https://www.w3schools.com/css/

w3schools. (2016). HTML5 HyperText Markup Language 5.
https://www.w3schools.com/html/

WAMP (2016). Wamp Server. http://www.wampserver.com/en/

ANNEXES

Annex A. Search engine and user counter

For this project a Gmail account was created and a registration was made at https://cse.google.es/cse/ to obtain the script that is inserted into the web page. PHP was used in the counter to keep track of users in each section of the site with a text file with txt extension and the code.

Figure 1. Specialised search engine.

```
<script>
  (function() {
    var cx = '010974444259289757554:-sggw2h8ixq';
    var gcse = document.createElement('script');
    gcse.type = 'text/javascript';
    gcse.async = true;
    gcse.src = (document.location.protocol == 'https:' ? 'https:' : 'http:')
        + '//cse.google.com/cse.js?cx=' + cx;
    var s = document.getElementsByTagName('script')[0];
    s.parentNode.insertBefore(gcse, s);
  })();
</script>
```

Figure 2. Search engine script code.

```
<?php
$maestro = fopen('container/contadorpri.rem','r+');//abrimos el archivo q cuenta los votos
$leer = fgets($maestro,20);//lo leemos
rewind($maestro);//ponemos el puntero al inicio del archivo
fputs($maestro,++$leer); //escribimos la linea leida mientras le aumentamos en uno
fclose($maestro);//cerramos el archivo
echo "CONTADOR :::: ", $leer, " ::::";//imprimimos en pantalla la
?>
```

Figure 3. PHP code for hit counter.

Annex B. Interface development

B. 1 Web text implementation

For the main page the html5 code tags were used and for the text the file was saved with an HTML extension for viewing in a web browser.

- html code for web development

```html
<!DOCTYPE html>
<html lang="es">
<head>
  <!-- Basic Page Needs
  ================================================== -->
      <meta charset="utf-8">
      <title>Centro de Documentación "Ecosistemas Litorales Mexicanos"</title>
  <!-- Mobile Specific Metas
  ================================================== -->
      <meta name="viewport" content="width=device-width, initial-scale=1, maximum-scale=1">
  <!-- CSS
  ================================================== -->
      <link rel="stylesheet" href="css/zerogrid.css">
      <link rel="stylesheet" href="css/style.css">
    <link rel="stylesheet" href="css/responsive.css">
      <link rel="stylesheet" href="css/responsiveslides.css" />
      <link href='./images/uam.ico' rel='icon' type='image/x-icon'/>
      <script src="js/jquery.min.js"></script>
      <script src="js/responsiveslides.js"></script>
      <script>
            $(function () {
              $("#slider").responsiveSlides({
                    auto: true,
                    pager: false,
                    nav: true,
                    speed: 500,
                    maxwidth: 962,
                    namespace: "centered-btns"
              });
            });


      </script>
</head>
<body>
<!-- -----------Header------------ -->
<header>
<div class="wrap-header zerogrid">
<div id="logo"><a href="index2.php"><img src="./images/logo_cdelm2.png"/></a></div>
<div         id="logo2"><a         href="http://www.iztapalapa.uam.mx/"         target="_black"><img
src="./images/logouamiorg.jpg"/></a></div>
                <div id="search">
<script>
 (function() {
   var cx = '010974444259289757554:-sggw2h8ixq';
   var gcse = document.createElement('script');
   gcse.type = 'text/javascript';
   gcse.async = true;
   gcse.src = (document.location.protocol == 'https:' ? 'https:' : 'http:') +
     '//cse.google.com/cse.js?cx=' + cx;
   var s = document.getElementsByTagName('script')[0];
   s.parentNode.insertBefore(gcse, s);
 })();
</script>
<gcse:searchbox-only></gcse:searchbox-only>

                </div>
        </div>
</header>
<nav>
        <div class="wrap-nav zerogrid">
                <div class="menu">
                        <ul>
```

```html
            </div>
        </div>
</header>
<nav>
        <div class="wrap-nav zerogrid">
                <div class="menu">
                        <ul>
                                <li class="first current"><a href="index2.php">CDELM</a></li>
                                <li><a href="objetivos.php">Objetivos</a></li>
                                <li><a href="blog.php">Publicaciones</a></li>
                                <li><a href="colaboraciones.php">Colaboraciones</a></li>
                                <li><a href="services.php">Servicios</a></li>
                                <li><a href="single.php">¿Quienes somos?</a></li>
                                <li class="last"><a href="contact.php">Contacto</a></li>
                        </ul>
                </div>
                <div class="minimenu"><div>MENU</div>
                        <select onchange="location=this.value">
                                <option></option>
                                <option value="index2.php">CDELM</option>
                            <option value="objetivos.php">Objetivos</option>
                                <option value="blog.php">Publicaciones</option>
                                <option value="colaboraciones.php">Colaboraciones</option>
                                <option value="services.php">Servicios</option>
                                <option value="single.php">¿Quienes Somos?</option>


                                <option value="contact.php">Contacto</option>
                        </select>
                </div>
        </div>
</nav>
<div class="featured">
        <div class="wrap-featured zerogrid">
                <div class="slider">
                        <div class="rslides_container">
                                <ul class="rslides" id="slider">
                                        <li><img src="images/slider/slider1.png"/></li>
                                        <li><img src="images/slider/slider2.png"/></li>
                                        <li><img src="images/slider/slider3.png"/></li>
                                        <li><img src="images/slider/slider4.png"/></li>
                                </ul>
                        </div>
                </div>
        </div>
</div>
<!-- ------------Content------------- -->
<section id="content">
        <div class="wrap-content zerogrid">
                <div class="row block01">
                        <div class="col-full">
                                <div class="wrap-col">
                                        <h2>¡ Bienvenido a CDELM !</h2>


                                        <p>El Centro de Documentación Ecosistemas Litorales
Mexicanos (CDELM) presenta bibliografía compilada por el grupo de trabajo del laboratorio de
Ecosistemas Costeros en el Departamento de Hidrobiología de la Universidad Autónoma
Metropolitana-Iztapalapa. Es el más extenso acervo de información científica sobre ecosistemas
costeros como son: lagunas costeras, estuarios, pantanos, bahías y ensenadas.</p>
                                        <p>El CDELM está constituido por un acervo informativo de
aproximadamente 6,200 referencias bibliográficas (con resumen anexo), incluidos todos los temas
científicos publicados acerca de estos ecosistemas. Un requisito indispensable de la información
capturada, es la de haber sido avalada en forma académica. Por esta razón, el banco de datos está
conformado: por artículos científicos, tesis de los diferentes grados, así como presentaciones en
congresos, reuniones y simposio de carácter científico, a nivel nacional e internacional; en cambio,
están excluidos los reportes técnicos y documentos afines.</p>
                                </div>
                        </div>
                </div>
                <div class="row block02">
                        <div class="col-1-3">
                                <div class="wrap-col box1">
                                        <div class="redondo">
                                        <img src="images/galeria.png" />
                                        </div>
                                        <h2>Galeria</h2>
                                        <br>
```

<a class="button" href="galeria_i.php">Accede</a>
</div>
</div>
<div class="col-1-3">
<div class="wrap-col box2">
<div class="redondo">
<img src="images/db.png" />
</div>
<h2>Base de Datos</h2>
<!--<p>Bienvenidos a la BD de los ecosistemas costeros mexicanos ! ....
.... patrocinado por el CDELM.
</p> -->

<a class="button" href="bd.php">Accede</a>
</div>
</div>
<div class="col-1-3">
<div class="wrap-col box3">
<div class="redondo">
<img src="images/contacto.png" />
</div>
<h2>Contacto</h2>
<!--   <p>Aquí se puede ubicar el sitio de la Universidad, cómo ponerse en comunicación con los
administradores y más... </p> -->

<a class="button" href="contact.php">Accede</a>
</div>
</div>
<div class="row block03">
<div class="col-2-3">
<div class="wrap-col">
<h2><a   href="index2.php">Proyecto   CDELM</a></h2>
<img src="images/about.jpg" />
<p>El   CDELM   es   un   proyecto   de   la   <a
href="http://cbs.izt.uam.mx/index.php?lang=es-ES" target="_blank"> División de Ciencias Biológicas y
de la Salud</a> de la <a href="http://www.iztapalapa.uam.mx/" target="_blank">Universidad Autónoma
Metropolitana - Iztapalapa. </a> La información del CDELM se somete a constante actualización.
Favor de citar y dar crédito a los autores del sitio, los compiladores y a los autores de los documentos
contenidos en la base de datos.</p>
</div>
</div>
<div class="col-1-3">
<div class="wrap-col">
<h2>Servicios</h2>
<ul>
<li><a href="galeria_i.php">Galeria</a></li>
<li><a href="bd.php">Base de datos</a></li>
<li><a href="contact.php">Contacto</a></li>

</ul>
</div>
</div>
</div>
<div class="row block04">
<div class="col-full">
<div class="wrap-col">
<h2>-</h2>
<div class="partners">
<a   href="http://cbs.izt.uam.mx/index.php?lang=es-ES"
target="_blank" ><img src="images/casadcbs.jpg" /></a>
<a   href="http://www.iztapalapa.uam.mx/"
target="_blank" ><img src="images/casauam.jpg" /></a>

</div>
</div>
</div>
</div>
</div>
</section>
<!-- ------------Footer------------- -->
<footer>
<div class="wrap-footer">
<div class="copyright">
<p></p>

```
    <p>El   <a   href="index2.php"   target="">CDELM</a>   es   un   proyecto   de   la   <a
href="http://www.iztapalapa.uam.mx/"  target="_blank">División  de  Ciencias  Biológicas  y  de  la
Salud</a> de la <a href="http://www.iztapalapa.uam.mx/" target="_blank">Universidad Autónoma
Metropolitana - Iztapalapa.</a> </p>
        <p>La información del CDELM se somete a constante actualización. Favor de citar y dar crédito
a los autores del sitio, los compiladores </p>
        <p>a los autores de los documentos contenidos en la base de datos. Copyright © 2016 UAM-I
</p>
                        <?php
                        $maestro = fopen('container/contadorpri.rem','r+');//abrimos el archivo q cuenta
los votos

                        $leer = fgets($maestro,20);//lo leemos
                        rewind($maestro);//ponemos el puntero al inicio del archivo
                        fputs($maestro,++$leer); //escribimos la línea leída mientras le
                aumentamos en uno
                        fclose($maestro);//cerramos el archivo
                        echo "CONTADOR ::: ", $leer, " ::: ";//imprimimos en pantalla la
                        ?>
                </div>
        </div>
</footer>
</body></html>
```

- Previous result in the browser after inserting the code

B.2 Implementation of style sheets

- Style sheet code

```
/* --------------------Reset-------------------- */
a,abbr,acronym,address,applet,article,aside,audio,b,blockquote,big,body,center,canvas,caption,cite,co
de,command,datalist,dd,del,details,dfn,dl,div,dt,em,embed,fieldset,figcaption,figure,font,footer,form,h1,
h2,h3,h4,h5,h6,header,hgroup,html,i,iframe,img,ins,kbd,keygen,label,legend,li,meter,nav,object,ol,outp
ut,p,pre,progress,q,s,samp,section,small,span,source,strike,strong,sub,sup,table,tbody,tfoot,thead,th,tr
,td,video,tt,u,ul,var{background:transparent;border:0                                             none;font-
size:100%;margin:0;padding:0;border:0;outline:0;vertical-align:top;}ol, ul {list-style:none;}blockquote, q
{quotes:none;}table,     table     td     {padding:0;border:none;border-collapse:collapse;}img     {vertical-
align:top;}embed {vertical-align:top;}
article, aside, audio, canvas, command, datalist, details, embed, figcaption, figure, footer, header,
hgroup, keygen, meter, nav, output, progress, section, source, video {display:block;}
mark, rp, rt, ruby, summary, time {display:inline;}
input, textarea {border:0; padding:0; margin:0; outline: 0;}
iframe {border:0; margin:0; padding:0;}
input, textarea, select {margin:0; padding:0px;}


/* --------------------Font-------------------- */
/* --------------------Style-------------------- */
html, body {width:100%; padding:0; margin:0;}



/* body {background: #345A34 url("../images/agua961.jpg");color: #949494;font: 14px/25px Arial,
Helvetica, sans-serif;}*/
body {
    background: #345A34 url("../images/fondohecho.png") no-repeat fixed center  ;
    -webkit-background-size: cover;
    -moz-background-size: cover;
    -o-background-size: cover;
    background-size: cover;
    color: #FFFFFF;font: 14px/25px Arial, Helvetica, sans-serif;
}
a{color: #CDD6D7;text-decoration: none;}
a:hover {color: #4AA9C3; text-decoration: none;}
/* ++++++++++++++++++++++++++++++ */
.clear{content: "\0020"; display: block; height: 0; clear: both; visibility: hidden; }
/* --------------------Header-------------------- */
header {}
header .wrap-header{height: 130px;}
header #logo {position:absolute; top:30px; width: 100%;}
header #logo2 {position:absolute; top:30px; left:350px; width: 100%;}
header #search {position: absolute;top: 80px; right:0px; width: 218px;z-index: 15;}
/* header .button-search {       position: absolute;      right: 0px;       background:
url('../images/button-search.png') center center no-repeat;      width: 28px;   height:   35px;cursor:
pointer;} */
```

```css
/* header #search input{background: #FFF;     padding: 1px 33px 1px 5px;     width: 182px;   height:
32px;   border: 1px solid #CCCCCC;   -webkit-border-radius: 3px;      -moz-border-radius:   3px;   -
khtml-border-radius: 3px;       border-radius: 3px;}
*/
/* -------------------------------------------- */
/* ------------------Navigation---------------- */
nav {margin-top:20px;}
nav .wrap-nav{height: 58px;background:url("../images/nav.jpg"); border:3px solid #555555;}

.menu ul {list-style: none;margin: 0;padding: 0;}
.menu  ul li{position: relative;float: left;padding: 17px 10px 10px 10px; border-right:1px solid #53b2c3;
border-left:1px solid #82ceda; background:url("../images/nav-transp.png"); }
.menu ul li.first{border-left:none !important}
.menu ul li.last{border-right:none !important}
.menu   ul li:hover, .menu .current {background:url("../images/nav-current.jpg"); border-right:#000000
1px solid; border-left:#000000 1px solid;}
.menu   ul li a {font-size: 18px; line-height:14px;color:#ffffff;display: block;padding: 6px 10px;margin-
bottom: 5px;z-index: 6;position: relative; font-family: Impact,Charcoal,sans-serif; font-weight: normal;}
.menu   ul li:hover a {}


.minimenu{display:none;}
.minimenu{position: relative;margin: 0px;background:#333333; border: 1px solid #CCC;}
.minimenu div{overflow: hidden;position: relative;font: 18px/40px 'PT Sans Narrow';color: #ffffff;text-
align:center;text-transform:uppercase;font-weight:bold;}
.minimenu select{position: absolute;top: 0px;left: 0px;width: 100%;height: 100%; opacity: 0;filter:
progid:DXImageTransform.Microsoft.Alpha(opacity=0);  cursor: pointer;}

.share{ float: right;}
.share ul{list-style: none;margin: 0;padding: 0;}
.share ul li{position:relative; float:left; padding-right:5px;}
/* ------------------Navigation---------------- */

.featured{margin:30px auto;}
.featured .wrap-featured{background:#333;}
.featured .wrap-featured .slider{}
/* ------------------Content------------------ */
#content {}
#content .wrap-content{}

.block01 {margin:20px 10px; padding:30px; border-bottom:1px dashed #CCC; border-top:1px dashed
#CCC;}
.block01     h2{text-align:center;     font-size:30px;      line-height:35px;      color:#ffffff,      font-family:
Impact,Charcoal,sans-serif; font-weight: normal;}
.block01 p{font-size:20px; text-align:center; line-height:25px;}
.block01 a{color:#5FBCCD;}

.block02 {margin:20px 10px; text-align:center;}
.block02 h2{font-size:24px; line-height:30px; color:#ffffff; font-family: Impact,Charcoal,sans-serif; font-
weight: normal;}


.block02 p{font-size:16px; margin: 20px 0px; }
.block02 a{font-size: 24px;  color: #ffffff; font-family: Impact,Charcoal,sans-serif; font-weight: normal;}
.block02 .box1{background: #4AA9C3; color: #B7DDE8; padding: 30px; border: 3px solid #555555;}
.block02 .box1 a:hover{color:#B7DDE8;}
.block02 .box2{background: #C0504D; color: #E5B9B8; padding: 30px; border: 3px solid #555555;}
.block02 .box2 a:hover{color:#E5B9B8;}
.block02 .box3{background: #9BBB59; color: #D6E3BC; padding: 30px; border: 3px solid #555555;}
.block02 .box3 a:hover{color:#D6E3BC;}

.block03 {margin:20px 10px;}
.block03   h2{font-size:24px;   line-height:30px;   color:   #ffffff;   margin-bottom:   20px;   font-family:
Impact,Charcoal,sans-serif; font-weight: normal;}
.block03 img{float:left; margin:0px 10px 10px 0px; border: 3px solid #555555;}
.block03 ul{list-style-type:none;}
.block03 ul li{border-left: 3px solid #E1E1E1; padding:5px; margin-bottom: 5px; padding-left: 10px;}
.block03 ul li:hover{border-left: 3px solid #4AA9C3;}

.block04 {margin:20px 10px;}
.block04   h2{font-size:24px;   line-height:30px;   color:   #ffffff;   margin-bottom:   20px;   font-family:
Impact,Charcoal,sans-serif; font-weight: normal;}
.block04 .partners a{display: block; float:left; margin: 0px 28px 10px 0px; position: relative;}
.block04 .partners a img{display:block; border:3px solid #555555;}
```

```css
.block{ margin:10px;}

#main-content{}
#main-content article{clear: both;}
#main-content article .heading{}
#main-content article .content{}
#main-content article a{color: #ffffff;}
#main-content article h2{font-size:20px; line-height:30px; color: #ffffff; margin-bottom: 20px; font-family:
Impact,Charcoal,sans-serif; font-weight: normal;}
#main-content article img{ float:left; margin:0px 10px 10px 0px; border: 3px solid #555555;}
#main-content article p{margin-bottom:10px;}
#main-content article .more{float: right; margin-bottom: 30px;}
#main-content article a.comments{cursor: pointer;color: #ffffff; display: inline-block; padding: 6px 12px
6px 12px; font-size: 18px; font-family: Impact,Charcoal,sans-serif; font-weight: normal;}

#sidebar{}
#sidebar .box{margin-bottom:20px;}
#sidebar .heading{}
#sidebar .heading h2{font-size:24px; line-height:30px; color: #ffffff; margin-bottom: 20px; font-family:
Impact,Charcoal,sans-serif; font-weight: normal;}
/* #sidebar .heading h2{font-size:24px; line-height:30px; color: #ffffff; margin-bottom: 20px; font-family:
Impact,Charcoal,sans-serif; font-weight: normal; text-transform: uppercase ;} */
#sidebar .content{padding:15px}
#sidebar .content img{float:left; margin:0px 10px 10px 0px; border: 3px solid #555555;}
#sidebar .content ul{list-style-type:none;}
.block{ margin:10px;}

#main-content{}
#main-content article{clear: both;}
#main-content article .heading{}
#main-content article .content{}
#main-content article a{color: #ffffff;}
#main-content article h2{font-size:20px; line-height:30px; color: #ffffff; margin-bottom: 20px; font-family:
Impact,Charcoal,sans-serif; font-weight: normal;}
#main-content article img{ float:left; margin:0px 10px 10px 0px; border: 3px solid #555555;}
#main-content article p{margin-bottom:10px;}
#main-content article .more{float: right; margin-bottom: 30px;}
#main-content article a.comments{cursor: pointer;color: #ffffff; display: inline-block; padding: 6px 12px
6px 12px; font-size: 18px; font-family: Impact,Charcoal,sans-serif; font-weight: normal;}

#sidebar{}
#sidebar .box{margin-bottom:20px;}
#sidebar .heading{}
#sidebar .heading h2{font-size:24px; line-height:30px; color: #ffffff; margin-bottom: 20px; font-family:
Impact,Charcoal,sans-serif; font-weight: normal;}
/* #sidebar .heading h2{font-size:24px; line-height:30px; color: #ffffff; margin-bottom: 20px; font-family:
Impact,Charcoal,sans-serif; font-weight: normal; text-transform: uppercase ;} */
#sidebar .content{padding:15px}
#sidebar .content img{float:left; margin:0px 10px 10px 0px; border: 3px solid #555555;}
#sidebar .content ul{list-style-type:none;}
.block{ margin:10px;}

#main-content{}
#main-content article{clear: both;}
#main-content article .heading{}
#main-content article .content{}
#main-content article a{color: #ffffff;}
#main-content article h2{font-size:20px; line-height:30px; color: #ffffff; margin-bottom: 20px; font-family:
Impact,Charcoal,sans-serif; font-weight: normal;}
#main-content article img{ float:left; margin:0px 10px 10px 0px; border: 3px solid #555555;}
#main-content article p{margin-bottom:10px;}
#main-content article .more{float: right; margin-bottom: 30px;}
#main-content article a.comments{cursor: pointer;color: #ffffff; display: inline-block; padding: 6px 12px
6px 12px; font-size: 18px; font-family: Impact,Charcoal,sans-serif; font-weight: normal;}

#sidebar{}
#sidebar .box{margin-bottom:20px;}
#sidebar .heading{}
#sidebar .heading h2{font-size:24px; line-height:30px; color: #ffffff; margin-bottom: 20px; font-family:
Impact,Charcoal,sans-serif; font-weight: normal;}
/* #sidebar .heading h2{font-size:24px; line-height:30px; color: #ffffff; margin-bottom: 20px; font-family:
Impact,Charcoal,sans-serif; font-weight: normal; text-transform: uppercase ;} */
#sidebar .content{padding:15px}
#sidebar .content img{float:left; margin:0px 10px 10px 0px; border: 3px solid #555555;}
#sidebar .content ul{list-style-type:none;}
```

```css
.block{ margin:10px;}

#main-content{}
#main-content article{clear: both;}
#main-content article .heading{}
#main-content article .content{}
#main-content article a{color: #ffffff;}
#main-content article h2{font-size:20px; line-height:30px; color: #ffffff; margin-bottom: 20px; font-family:
Impact,Charcoal,sans-serif; font-weight: normal;}
#main-content article img{ float:left; margin:0px 10px 10px 0px; border: 3px solid #555555;}
#main-content article p{margin-bottom:10px;}
#main-content article .more{float: right; margin-bottom: 30px;}
#main-content article a.comments{cursor: pointer;color: #ffffff; display: inline-block; padding: 6px 12px
6px 12px; font-size: 18px; font-family: Impact,Charcoal,sans-serif; font-weight: normal;}

#sidebar{}
#sidebar .box{margin-bottom:20px;}
#sidebar .heading{}
#sidebar .heading h2{font-size:24px; line-height:30px; color: #ffffff; margin-bottom: 20px; font-family:
Impact,Charcoal,sans-serif; font-weight: normal;}
/* #sidebar .heading h2{font-size:24px; line-height:30px; color: #ffffff; margin-bottom: 20px; font-family:
Impact,Charcoal,sans-serif; font-weight: normal; text-transform: uppercase ;} */
#sidebar .content{padding:15px}
#sidebar .content img{float:left; margin:0px 10px 10px 0px; border: 3px solid #555555;}
#sidebar .content ul{list-style-type:none;}


#sidebar .content ul li{border-left: 3px solid #E1E1E1; margin-bottom: 5px; padding-left: 10px ; margin-
left: 5px;}
#sidebar .content ul li:hover{border-left: 3px solid #4AA9C3;}
#sidebar .content .post { margin-bottom: 20px;}
#sidebar .content .post h4{ font-size:14px; font-weight:normal;}
#sidebar .content .post img{ float:left; border: 3px solid #555555; margin-right:10px;}
#sidebar .content .post p{color:#A3A3A3; font-style:italic;}
/* ------------------------------------------ */
/* ------------------Footer------------------ */
footer {background-color:#333;}
.wrap-footer{}
.copyright{text-align:center; background:#333333; padding:10px 0px;color:#ffffff; }
.copyright a{text-decoration:underline; color:#ffffff; }

/* ------------------------------------------ */
/* -----------------Components------------------ */
.photos{}
.photos:after{content: "\0020"; display: block; height: 0; clear: both; visibility: hidden; }
.photos a{display: block; float:left; margin: 0px 4px 10px 4px;position: relative;}
.photos a img{display:block; border:1px solid #CCC;}

#pagi{margin: 50px auto; padding: 30px 0px;list-style: none;width: 250px;}
#pagi li {float: left;margin-right: 10px;}
#pagi li a {display: block;          text-decoration: none; color: #717171;font: bold 16px Arial, sans-
serif;padding: 10px 13px; background: #ffffff;}
#pagi li a.current, #pagi li a:hover {color: #ffffff;  background: #4AA9C3;}


.comment{font-weight:bold; margin:50px 0px; width: auto;}
.comment div{margin-bottom: 20px; vertical-align:middle; }
.comment input{border: 2px solid #999999;padding: 8px 10px;width:250px;}
.comment textarea{border: 2px solid #999999;padding: 8px 10px;width:95%;}
.comment input[type="submit"] {cursor: pointer; width:100px; float:right;
        background: -webkit-linear-gradient(top, #efefef, #ddd);background: -moz-linear-gradient(top,
#efefef, #ddd);
        background: -ms-linear-gradient(top, #efefef, #ddd);background: -o-linear-gradient(top, #efefef,
#ddd);
        background: linear-gradient(top, #efefef, #ddd);
        color: #333;text-shadow: 0px 1px 1px rgba(255,255,255,1);       border: 2px solid #999999;}
.comment input[type="submit"]:hover {
        background: -webkit-linear-gradient(top, #eee, #ccc);   background:  -moz-linear-gradient(top,
#eee, #ccc);
        background: -ms-linear-gradient(top, #eee, #ccc);       background:       -o-linear-gradient(top,
#eee, #ccc);
        background: linear-gradient(top, #eee, #ccc);   border: 2px solid #bbb;}
.comment input[type="submit"]:active {
        background: -webkit-linear-gradient(top, #ddd, #aaa);   background:  -moz-linear-gradient(top,
#ddd, #aaa);
        background: -ms-linear-gradient(top, #ddd, #aaa);       background:       -o-linear-gradient(top,
#ddd, #aaa);
```

```css
        background: linear-gradient(top, #ddd, #aaa);    border: 2px solid #999;}

/* +++++++++++++++++++++++++++++++++++++++++++++++++++++++++++++++ BOTONES  NUEVOS
++++++++++++++++++++++++++++++++++ */
a.button {
  border-top: 1px solid #96d1f8;
  background: #65a9d7;
  background: -webkit-gradient(linear, left top, left bottom, from(#3e779d), to(#65a9d7));
  background: -webkit-linear-gradient(top, #3e779d, #65a9d7);
  background: -moz-linear-gradient(top, #3e779d, #65a9d7);
  background: -ms-linear-gradient(top, #3e779d, #65a9d7);
  background: -o-linear-gradient(top, #3e779d, #65a9d7);
  padding: 8px 16px;
  -webkit-border-radius: 9px;
  -moz-border-radius: 9px;
  border-radius: 9px;
  -webkit-box-shadow: rgba(0,0,0,1) 0 1px 0;
  -moz-box-shadow: rgba(0,0,0,1) 0 1px 0;
  box-shadow: rgba(0,0,0,1) 0 1px 0;
  text-shadow: rgba(0,0,0,.4) 0 1px 0;
  color: white;
  font-size: 18px;
  font-family: 'Lucida Grande', Helvetica, Arial, Sans-Serif;
  text-decoration: none;
  vertical-align: middle;
  }
a.button:hover {
  border-top-color: #28597a;
  background: #28597a;
  color: #ccc;
  }


a.button:active {
  border-top-color: #1b435e;
  background: #1b435e;
  }
/* ------------------------------ Imágenes redondeando ------------------------------ */
.redondo img {
border: 2px solid grey;
margin: 0;
padding: 0;
border-radius: 800px;
overflow: hidden;
}
```

Annex C. Installation of WAMP

The process consists of 11 simple steps:

1. Download the installation file from the website
http://www.wampserver.es/. Windows automatically installs PHP version
5.4.3, Apache version 2.2.22 and MySQL version 5.5.24.

2. Start of the installation process.

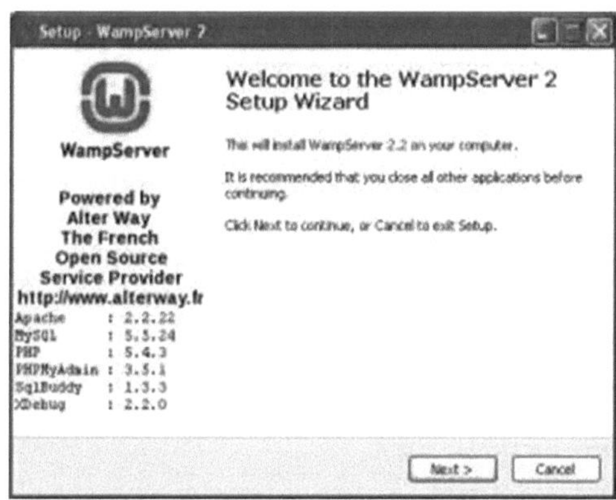

3. Click the "Next" button to display the WAMP Server license.

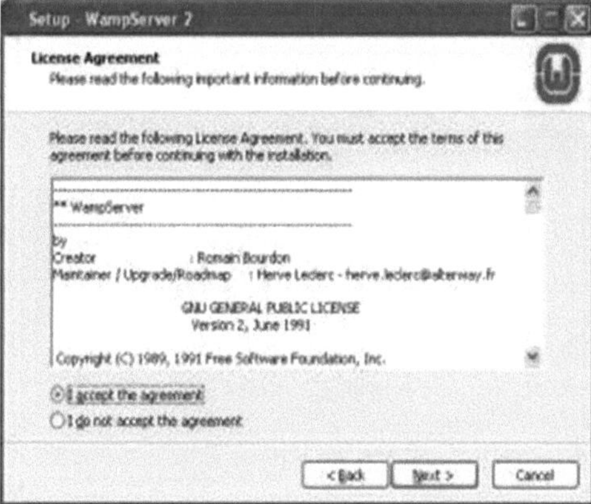

4. Selection of the directory for server installation.

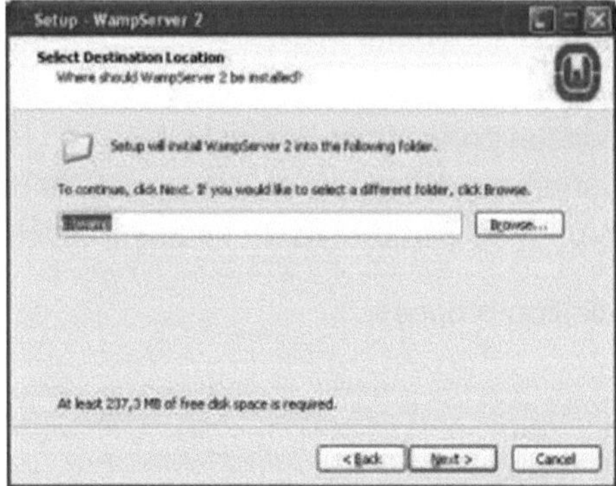

5. Default icon creation "Create a Quick Launch icon".

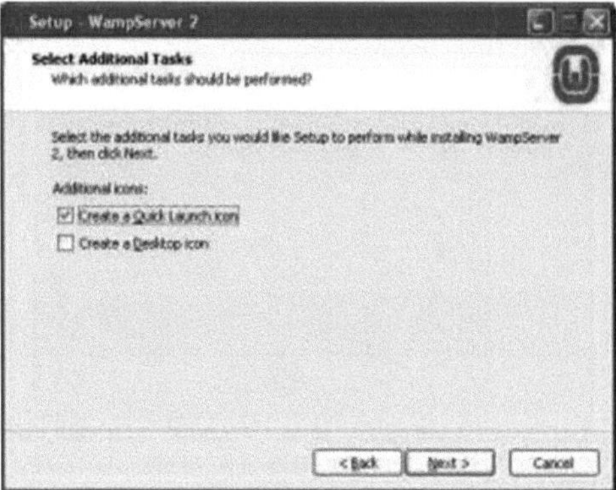

6. Installation overview.

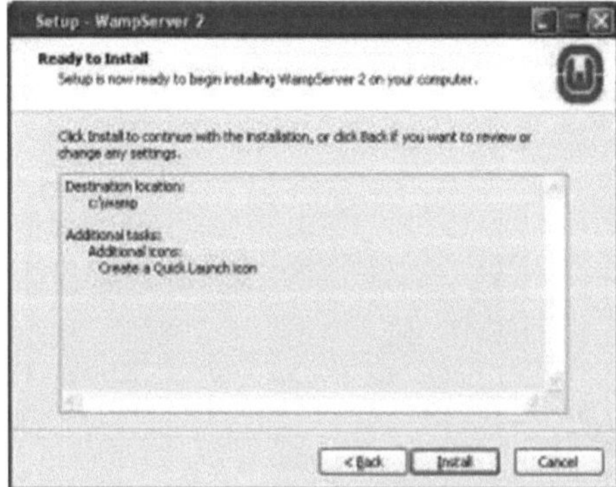

7. Installation of the WAMP Server.

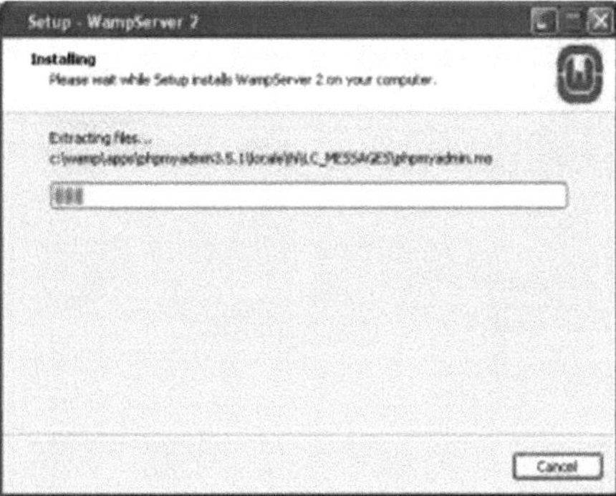

8. Search for the directory where the server is installed.

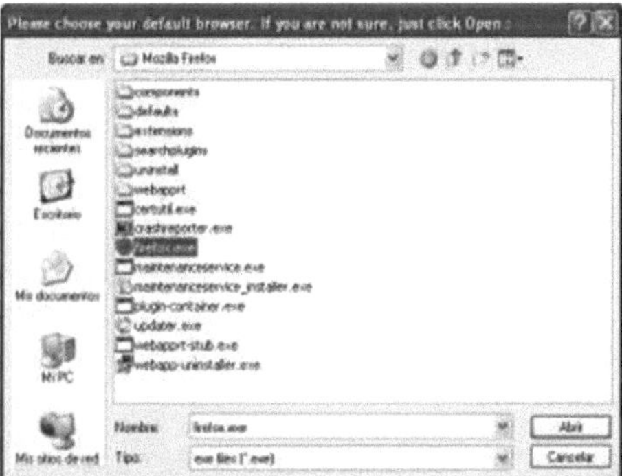

9. Grant permissions for Apache and unlock it. Configure SMTP settings by typing "localhost" and an email.

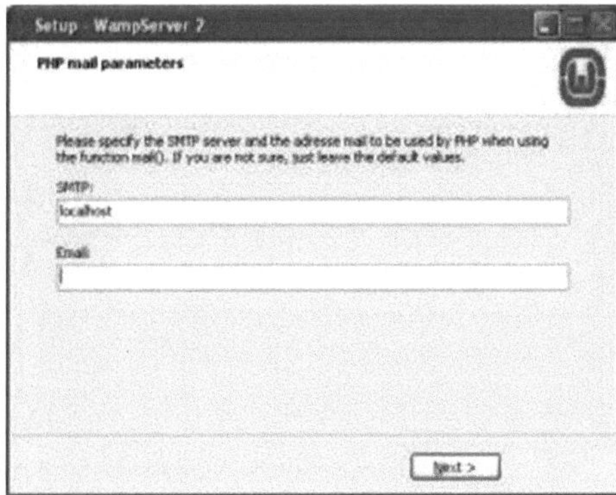

10. Finish installing WAMP Server. Click "Launch WampServer 2 now" if you want it to run after installation.

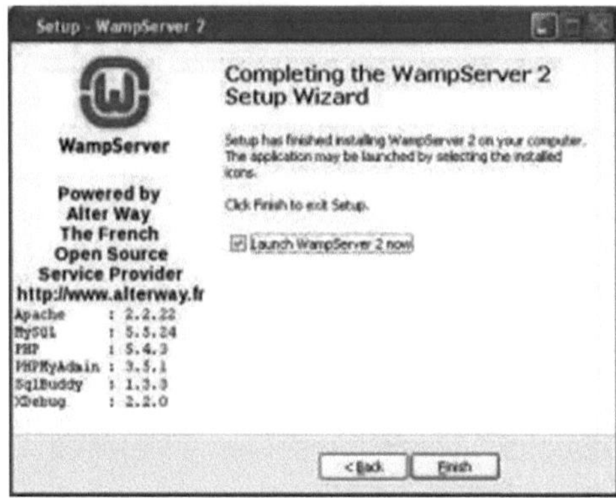

11. Accessing from the browser to the following address http://localhost you will find the following image that shows that WAMPServer is correctly installed and working.

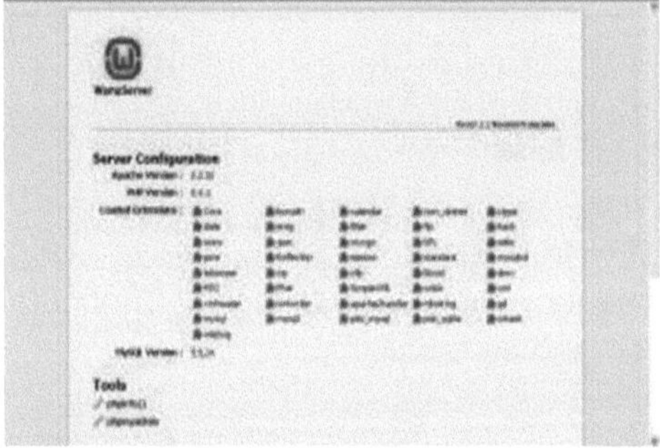

I want morebooks!

Buy your books fast and straightforward online - at one of world's fastest growing online book stores! Environmentally sound due to Print-on-Demand technologies.

Buy your books online at
www.morebooks.shop

Kaufen Sie Ihre Bücher schnell und unkompliziert online – auf einer der am schnellsten wachsenden Buchhandelsplattformen weltweit! Dank Print-On-Demand umwelt- und ressourcenschonend produziert.

Bücher schneller online kaufen
www.morebooks.shop

info@omniscriptum.com
www.omniscriptum.com

Printed by Books on Demand GmbH, Norderstedt / Germany